# The No-Go King

## Exodus 5–15

### (The Exodus)

## Mary Manz Simon

## Illustrated by Dennis Jones

SAINT LOUIS

# For Lo Simon
## Mark 10:14

### Books by Mary Manz Simon

**Hear Me Read Level 1**
*What Next?* CPH
*Drip Drop,* CPH
*Jibber Jabber,* CPH
*Hide the Baby,* CPH
*Toot! Toot!* CPH
*Bing!* CPH
*Whoops!* CPH
*Send a Baby,* CPH
*A Silent Night,* CPH
*Follow That Star,* CPH
*Row the Boat,* CPH
*Rumble, Rumble,* CPH
*Who Will Help?* CPH
*Sit Down,* CPH
*Come to Jesus,* CPH
*Too Tall, Too Small,* CPH
*Hurry, Hurry!* CPH
*Where Is Jesus?* CPH

**Hear Me Read Level 2**
*The No-Go King,* CPH
*Hurray for the Lord's Army!* CPH
*The Hide-and-Seek Prince,* CPH
*Daniel and the Tattletales,* CPH
*The First Christmas,* CPH
*Through the Roof,* CPH
*A Walk on the Waves,* CPH
*Thank You,* Jesus, CPH

*God's Children Pray,* CPH
*My First Diary,* CPH
*52 Ways to Raise Happy, Loving Kids*
   Thomas Nelson Publishing

*Little Visits on the Go,* CPH
*Little Visits 1-2-3,* CPH
*Little Visits with Jesus,* CPH
*More Little Visits with Jesus,* CPH

Copyright © 1993 Concordia Publishing House
3558 S. Jefferson Avenue, St. Louis, MO 63118-3968
Manufactured in the United States of America

Library of Congress Cataloging-in-Publication Data

Simon, Mary Manz, 1948–
      The no-go king: Exodus 5-15: the Exodus / Mary Manz Simon: illustrated by Dennis Jones.
         p.     cm. — (Hear me read. Level 2)
      Summary: A simple retelling of the Bible story in which Moses leads the children of Israel out of slavery in Egypt.
      ISBN 0-570-04732-3
      1. Exodus. The—Juvenile literature. 2. Bible stories. English—O.T. Exodus. [1. Exodus, The. 2. Moses (Biblical Leader) 3. Bible stories—O.T.] I. Jones, Dennis, ill. II. Title III. Title: Exodus. IV. Series: Simon, Mary Manz, 1948— Hear me read. Level 2.
BS680.E9S56   1993
222'.1209505—dc20                                                      92-31888

3   4   5   6   7   8   9   10      02   01   00   99   98

God's people were sad.
They wanted to go to the Promised Land.
The king would not let them go.

"No," said the king.
"You cannot go.
You must work."

So God's people worked.
They worked and worked and worked.

Moses said, "God's people want to go.
Let the people go."

But the king said, "No.
The people must work.
The people cannot go."

God sent frogs to punish the king.
Frogs jumped everywhere.

"Jump, frogs, jump!" God's people
shouted.
"Now the king will let us go."

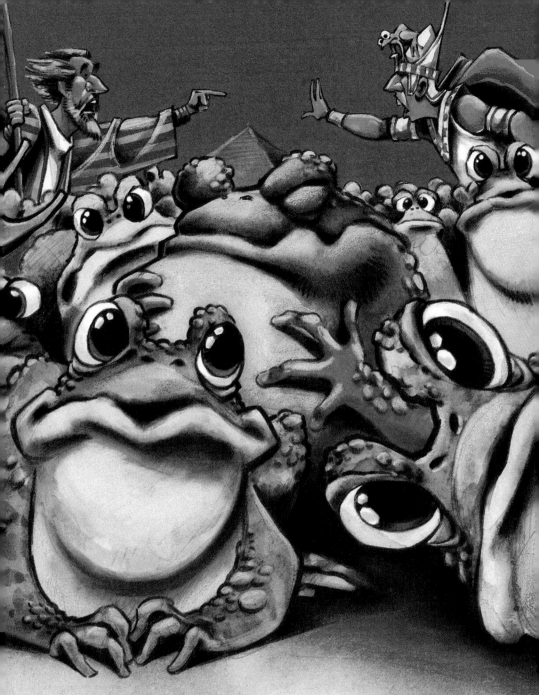

So Moses said to the king, "Let God's people go."

But the king said, "No. The people cannot go."

God sent bugs to punish the king.
Bugs flew everywhere.
"Shoo, fly, shoo," God's people shouted.
"Now the king will let us go."

So Moses said to the king, "Let God's people go."

But the king said, "No.
The people cannot go."

God punished the king again.
God punished the king again and again
and again.
God sent one last punishment.
Some of the king's people died.

"Let God's people go," said Moses.

"Go," said the king.

"We are free to go," said Moses.
"The king said, 'Go!'"

"We are free at last.
Thank You, God," said the people.
"We are free at last."

The people walked and walked.
Some carried pans of bread.
Some carried gold and silver jewelry.
Everybody was happy.

"The king said, 'Go'; so here we go.
We are going to the Promised Land,"
sang the people.

"Hurry up," said the people. "Hurry up!"

The sheep and cows walked.
The goats kicked.
Even the animals could go to the Promised Land.

Then Moses told the people, "God said, 'Stop.'
We will stop here."
The people camped by the Red Sea.

But the people saw something.
"Look!" they said.
It was a cloud of dust.
The king's chariots were chasing them.

"Where can we go?" asked the people.
They looked ahead.
They saw the Red Sea.
They looked behind.
The chariots were coming.

The people looked at Moses.

Moses said, "Don't be afraid.
Trust in God.
God will help us."

God said to Moses, "Hold your hand over the Red Sea."
The water went back.
The Red Sea opened up.

Now the people could go to the Promised Land.

"Hurry up," said the people.
"Hurry up!"

The people walked.
The people walked quickly.
Some people carried pans of bread.
Some people carried gold and silver
jewelry.

"The king said, 'Go.' So here we go. We are going to the Promised Land," sang the people.

The sheep and cows walked.
The goats kicked.
Even the animals could go to the Prom-
ised Land.

"Hurry up," said the people.
"Hurry up!"

"We are free," said the people.
"Thank You, God," they said.
"We are free at last."